Figure Skating

by Julie Murray

Abdo
ARTISTIC SPORTS
Kids

Abdo Kids Jumbo is an Imprint of Abdo Kids
abdobooks.com

abdobooks.com

Published by Abdo Kids, a division of ABDO, P.O. Box 398166, Minneapolis, Minnesota 55439. Copyright © 2023 by Abdo Consulting Group, Inc. International copyrights reserved in all countries. No part of this book may be reproduced in any form without written permission from the publisher. Abdo Kids Jumbo™ is a trademark and logo of Abdo Kids.

Printed in the United States of America, North Mankato, Minnesota.

102022
012023

Photo Credits: Alamy, AP Images, Getty Images, Granger Collection, Shutterstock PREMIER

Production Contributors: Teddy Borth, Jennie Forsberg, Grace Hansen
Design Contributors: Candice Keimig, Pakou Moua

Library of Congress Control Number: 2022937183
Publisher's Cataloging-in-Publication Data

Names: Murray, Julie, author.

Title: Figure skating / by Julie Murray

Description: Minneapolis, Minnesota : Abdo Kids, 2023 | Series: Artistic sports | Includes online resources and index.

Identifiers: ISBN 9781098264222 (lib. bdg.) | ISBN 9781098264789 (ebook) | ISBN 9781098265069 (Read-to-Me ebook)

Subjects: LCSH: Figure skating--Juvenile literature. | Ice skating--Juvenile literature. | Winter sports--Juvenile literature. | Sports--Juvenile literature. | Sports--History--Juvenile literature.

Classification: DDC 796.912--dc23

Table of Contents

Figure Skating 4	More Facts 22
History. 6	Glossary 23
Skates and Costumes 12	Index 24
Types of Figure Skating 16	Abdo Kids Code. 24

Figure Skating

Figure skating is a sport that requires **artistic** and athletic skills. Skaters perform a **choreographed** routine. It is set to music.

5

History

Skating first appeared in Finland in around 3000 BCE. People used animal bones as skate blades. These allowed skaters to travel across frozen lakes.

Figure skating evolved in the 1860s. Jackson Haines was an American ballet dancer. He had ice skaters perform ballet moves. The moves were set to music.

Jackson Haines

Today, figure skating is one of the most popular Olympic sports. Skaters from around the world compete at the Winter Olympics every four years.

Skates and Costumes

Skate boots are made of leather. The blades are made of steel and have toe picks at the fronts. The **jagged** edges allow skaters to perform jumps.

Figure skaters wear special costumes. The costumes are often beaded and sparkly. Pairs wear costumes that go well together.

Types of Figure Skating

There are four types of figure skating. They are singles, pairs, ice dancing, and **synchronized skating**.

16

In singles, skaters perform alone. Couples perform together in pairs skating. Both types include jumps and spins. Pairs also do lifts.

Ice dancing is also done in pairs, but no jumps are performed. It is more focused on body movements. Groups of skaters perform together in **synchronized skating**.

More Facts

- Figure skating was the first winter sport in the Olympics. It was part of the 1908 Olympics in London.

- Skaters are scored in five categories on a scale from 0 to 10. The categories are skills, transitions, performance, composition, and interpretation.

- When skaters spin, they reach fast speeds! They can complete 300 **revolutions** per minute (RPM)!

Glossary

artistic – having to do with the arts.

choreographed – to have planned the movements of a single routine.

jagged – having points that are sharp and uneven.

revolution – the rotation of a body on its axis. One revolution is equal to one full spin.

synchronized skating – an ice-skating sport where between 8 and 16 skaters perform together as a team. They move as a flowing unit at high speed while performing elements and footwork.

Index

costume 14

Finland 6

Haines, Jackson 8

history 6, 8

ice dancing 16, 20

jumps 12, 18, 20

lifts 18

music 4, 8

pairs 14, 16, 18, 20

routine 4

singles 16, 18

skates 6, 12

skills 4

spins 18

synchronized skating 16, 20

types 16

Winter Olympics 10

Visit abdokids.com to access crafts, games, videos, and more!

Use Abdo Kids code AFK4222 or scan this QR code!